THE BEST OF

STING

GW00458376

FIELDS OF GOLD

1984-1994

Magnetic Publishing Limited

Exclusive Distributors:

Music Sales Limited
8/9 Frith Street,
London W1V 5TZ, England.

Music Sales Pty Limited
120 Rothschild Avenue,
Rosebery, NSW 2018,
Australia.

Order No. AM928070
ISBN 0-7119-4876-3
This book © Copyright 1994 by
Magnetic Publishing Limited.

Your Guarantee of Quality:
As publishers, we strive to produce every
book to the highest commercial standards.
Whilst endeavouring to retain the original
running order of the recorded album,
this book has been carefully designed to
minimise awkward page turns and to make
playing from it a real pleasure.

Particular care has been given to specifying
acid-free, neutral-sized paper made from pulps
which have not been elemental chlorine bleached.
This pulp is from farmed sustainable
forests and was produced with special regard
for the environment.

Throughout, the printing and
binding have been planned to ensure a
sturdy, attractive publication which should
give years of enjoyment.

If your copy fails to meet
our high standards, please inform us and
we will gladly replace it.

Music Sales' complete catalogue
describes thousands of titles and is
available in full colour sections by subject,
direct from Music Sales Limited.
Please state your areas of interest and send a
cheque/postal order for £1.50 for postage to:
Music Sales Limited, Newmarket Road,
Bury St. Edmunds, Suffolk IP33 3YB.

Printed in the United Kingdom by
Caligraving Limited,
Thetford, Norfolk.

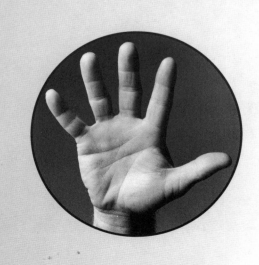

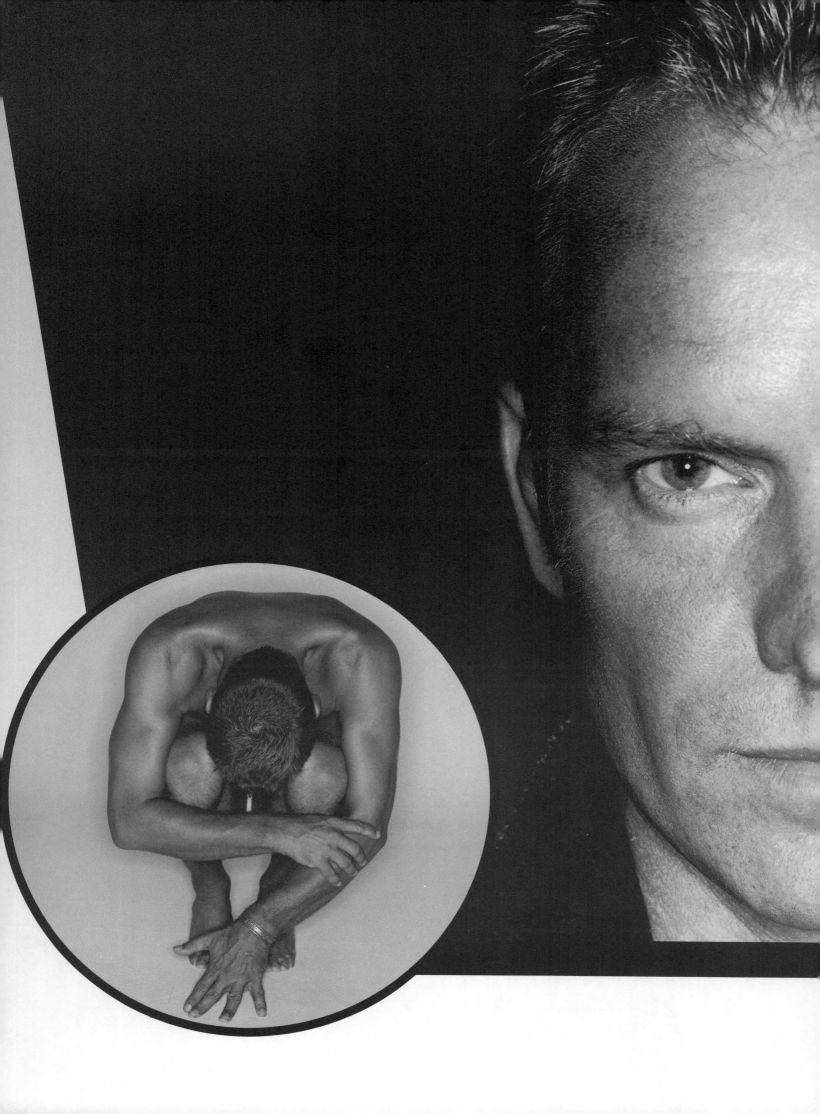

WHEN WE DANCE

Words & Music by Sting

If he loved you like I love you, I would walk a-way in shame, I'd move town, I'd change my name. When he

watch- es you,—   when— he   counts to buy your soul
2. The priest has said my soul's— sal - va - tion,   is   in the ba - lance of—

on— your   hand his gold - en rings,   like— he
— the an - gels   and un - der- neath   the wheels— of   pas - sion

owns   a bird that sings.
I keep the faith   in my— fash - ion.}   When— we

dance   an - gels   will   run and hide— their
(2ª) I'm gon- na love you more than life,   if you'll   on - ly   be   my   wife.—

8

wings.

1.

wings.
I'm gon-na love you night and day,

When we dance, an-gels will run and hide— their
I'm gon-na try in ev-'ry way. I'm gon-na find a place to live, give you all I've got to give.

wings.
I will love you more than life if you will on-ly be my wife.

If I could break down— these walls— and shout my name at hea-ven's gate

love you— he— won't care for you this way,

he'll— mis - treat you if you stay. Come— and

live with me,— we'll— have child- ren of our own,

I— would love you more than life, if— you

come and be my wife.
I'm gon-na love you more than life, if you will on-ly be my wife. When— we

dance an - gels will run and hide their
I'm gon-na love you night and day, I'm gon-na try in ev-'ry way.
I'm gon-na find a place to live, give you all I've got to give.

wings.
I'm gon-na find a place to live, give you all I've got to give.
I'm gon-na love you more than life, if you will on-ly be my wife. When— we

dance an - gels will run and hide their
I'm gon-na love you more than life, if you will on-ly be my wife.

12

13

IF YOU LOVE SOMEBODY SET THEM FREE

Words & Music by Sting

Set them free.

If it's a mirror you want,

(_____ them free)   (Free, free, set _____ them free)

_____ them free)   You can't con-

trol an in-de-pen-dent heart,

(can't love what you can't keep)

Can't tear the one you love a-part.

(can't love what you

FIELDS OF GOLD

Words & Music by Sting

Man - y   years have passed   since those_
mem - ber   me   when the _

_ sum-mer days   a - mong   the fields _ of bar - ley.   See the
_ west wind moves   up - on   the fields _ of bar - ley.   You can

ALL THIS TIME

Words & Music by Sting

1. I looked out a-cross

the ri-ver to-day,

CHORUS

All_____ this time_____ the

ri - ver flowed____ end - less - ly to the sea..

1.
2. Two priests If_ I had_ my way,_

I'd take a boat from the ri - ver___ and I'd bu - ry

To Coda

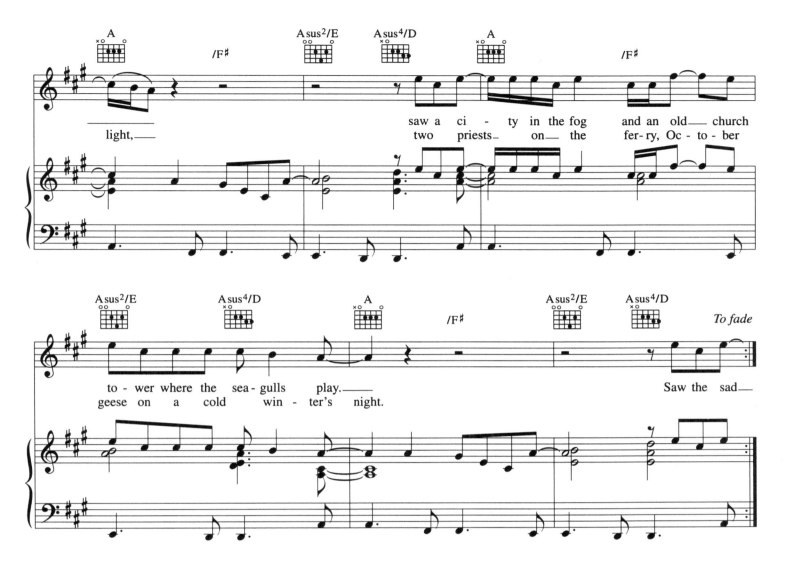

Verse 2:

Two priests came round our house tonight
One young, one old, to offer prayers for the dying,
  to serve the final rite
One to learn, one to teach
Which way the cold wind blows
Fussing and flapping in priestly black
Like a murder of crows.

Chorus:

Verse 3:

Blessed are the poor, for they shall inherit the earth
Better to be poor than be a fat man in the eye of the needle
And as these words were spoken I swear I hear
The old man laughing
What good is a used up world,
And how could it be worth having.

Chorus 3:

All this time the river flowed
Endlessly like a silent tear
And all this time the river flowed
Father, if Jesus exists then how come He never lived here.

AN ENGLISHMAN IN NEW YORK

Words & Music by Sting

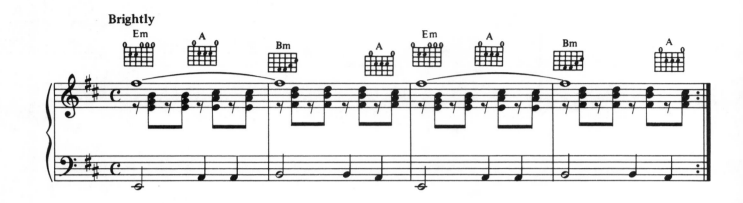

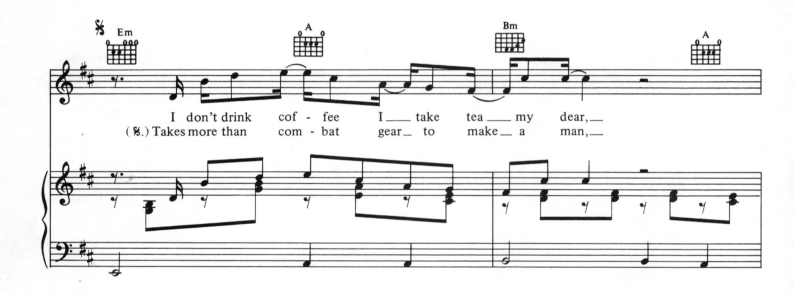

I don't drink cof-fee I__ take tea__ my dear,__
(%.) Takes more than com-bat gear__ to make__ a man,__

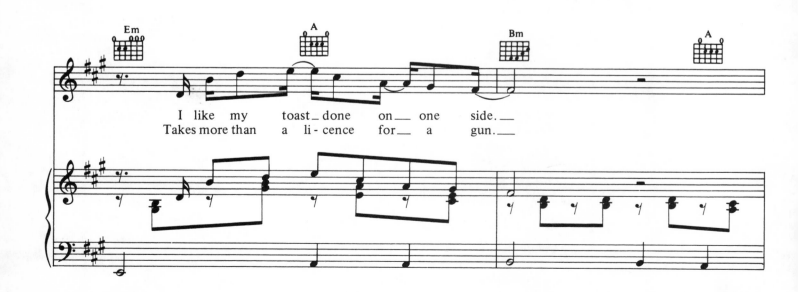

I like my toast__ done on__ one side.__
Takes more than a li-cence for__ a gun.__

Gen-tle - ness, __ so - bri - e - ty, are

rare in this so - ci - e - ty, at night a can-dle's bright-er than __ the sun. __

Solo ad lib.

MAD ABOUT YOU

Words & Music by Sting

This song is in A minor for ease of playing.
The recording from which it was transcribed is in A♭ minor.

A stone's throw from Je - ru - sa - lem

I walked a lone - ly mile in the moon - light. And though a mil - lion stars— were shin - ing,

To Coda ⊕

my heart was lost on a dis - tant pla - net that whirls a - round the A - pril moon,

whirl - ing in an arc of sad - ness, I'm lost with - out you,— I'm lost with - out you.— Though

all my king - doms turn— to sand— and fall in - to— the sea,— I'm mad a - bout— you,——— I'm

mad a - bout— you.———

And from the dark se - clu - ded val - leys
They say a city in the de - sert lies——

IT'S PROBABLY ME

Words & Music by Sting, Eric Clapton & Michael Kamen

1. If the night turned— cold
(Verse 2 see block lyric)
and the stars— looked— down
and you hug— your-

self
on the cold— cold— ground,
you wake— the morn-ing
in a stran-ger's

coat,
no one would you
see.
You ask— your-

self,   who'd watch for me,   my on - ly friend,   who could it be?___

___ It's hard_ to say it,   I hate   to say it   but it's pro - bab - ly

me._   2. When your bel - ly's   You're not the

ea - si - est per - son I   ev - er got to know   and it's hard for us both_ to let our

feel-ings show,   some would say   I should let_ you go your way, you'll on-ly make me cry._

But if there's one guy,_   just_

_ one guy,   who'd lay down_ his life for you and die,_   I hate_ to

say it,   I hate   to say it,   but it's pro-bab-ly me._

Verse 2:

When your belly's empty and the hunger's so real
And you're too proud to beg and too dumb to steal,
You search the city for your only friend,
No one would you see.
You ask yourself, who could it be?
A solitary voice to speak out and set you free.
I hate to say it, I hate to say it
But it's probably me.

THEY DANCE ALONE

Words & Music by Sting

(1.) Why are these wo-men here,___ danc-ing on their own?

[Verses 2 & 3 see under]

Why is there this sad - ness in their eyes?___

Why are the sol-diers here, ____ their fa-ces fixed like stone?

I can't see what it is that they ___ des - pise. ____

They're danc-ing with the miss-ing, ___ they're danc-ing with the dead, ____

they dance with the in - vi - si - ble ones, ___ their an-guish is un - said.

They're danc-ing with their fa - thers,   they're danc-ing with their sons,

they're danc-ing with their hus-bands,   they dance a - lone,   they dance a -

lone.   One day we'll dance on their graves,   one __ day we'll sing our free - dom.

One __ day we'll laugh in our joy,   and we'll dance. __

One day we'll dance on their graves, one___ day we'll sing our free - dom.

One___ day we'll laugh in our joy, and we'll dance.___

Ellas danzan con los desaparecidos, danzan con los muertos, danzan con amores invisibles.

Con silenciosa angistia, danzan con sus padres, con sus hijos, con sus esposos. Ellas danzan solos, danzan solos.

VERSE 2:
The only form of protest they're allowed
I've seen their silent faces, they scream so loud
If they were to speak these words, they'd go missing too
Another woman on the torture table, what else can they do?

VERSE 3:
Hey Mister Pinochet, you've sown a bitter crop
It's foreign money that supports you, one day the money's going to stop
No wages for your torturers, no budget for your guns
You think of your own mother dancing with her invisible son.

FRAGILE

Words & Music by Sting

If blood will flow when flesh and steel are one, dry-ing in the col-our of the even-ing sun. To-mor-row's rain will wash the stains a-way, but some-thing in our minds will al-ways stay. Per-

haps this fi - nal act ___ was meant ___ to clinch a life - time's ar - gu - ment that

no - thing comes ___ from vi - o - lence and no - thing e - ver could. ___ For

all those born ___ be - neath ___ an an - gry star, lest

we for - get ___ how fra - gile we are.

On ___ and on ___ the rain ___ will fall ___ like tears from ___ a star, ___ like tears from ___ a star ___ on ___ and on ___ the rain ___ will say ___ how fra - gile ___ we are, ___ how fra - gile ___ we are. ___

Solo ad lib.

59

IF I EVER LOSE MY FAITH IN YOU

Words & Music by Sting

You could say I
Some would say I was a
I nev-er saw no

lost my faith in sci-
lost man in a lost
mir-a-cle of sci-ence

ence
world.
and prog-ress.

I could be lost in - side their

lies with - out a trace, but ev -'ry

time I close my eyes I see your face.

D.S. al Coda

CODA

that did-n't al-ways end up as some-thing worse, but

WE'LL BE TOGETHER

Words & Music by Sting

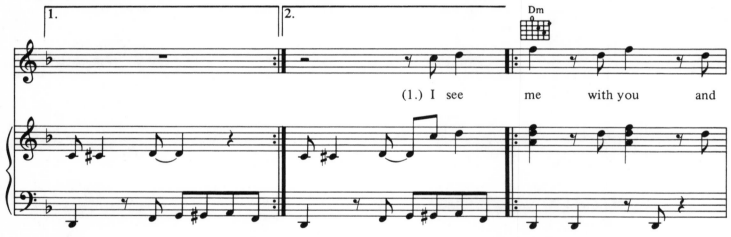

(1.) I see me with you and

all the things you do____ keep turn-ing round and round in my mind.____

We'll be to - ge - ther, we'll be to -

ge - ther, we'll be to - ge - ther.

To Coda ⊕

1.
2.

(2.) I see

Call me ba - by,

you can call me a - ny - thing you want.

VERSE 2:
I see you with me
And all I want to be
Is dancing here with you in my arms
Forget the weather
We should always be together
I'll always be a slave to your charms.

To have you with me I would swim the seven seas
I need you as my guide and my light
My love is a flame that burns in your name
We'll be together tonight.

VERSE 3:
I see you with me
And baby makes three . . .
I see me with you
And all the things we do . . .
Forget the weather we should always be together
I need you as my guide and my light
My love is a flame that burns in your name
We'll be together, we'll be together tonight.

NOTHING 'BOUT ME

Words & Music by Sting

Lay my head___ on a sur-geon's ta-ble.
Run my name___ through your com-put-er.

Take my fin-ger-prints___ if you___ are a-ble.
Men-tion me in pass-ing to your col-lege tu-tor.

74

LOVE IS THE SEVENTH WAVE

Words & Music by Sting

3. Feel it rising in the cities,
   Feel it sweeping over land,
   Over borders, over frontiers;
   Nothing will it's power withstand I say,
   There is no deeper wave than this
   Rising in the world.
   There is no deeper wave than this.
   Listen to me, girl.

4. All the bloodshed, all the anger,
   All the weapons, all the greed,
   All the armies, all the missiles,
   All the symbols of our fear I say
   There is a deeper wave than this
   Rising in the world.
   There is a deeper wave than this.
   Listen to me, girl.

5. At the still point of destruction,
   At the centre of the fury;
   All the angels, all the devils
   All around us, can't you see?
   There is a deeper wave than this
   Rising in the land.
   There is a deeper wave than this,
   Nothing will withstand.

RUSSIANS

Words & Music by Sting

So - vi - ets. Mis - ter Krush - chev said, "We will bu - ry you." I

don't sub - scribe to this point of view. It'd be such an ig - nor - ant

thing to do___ if the Rus - sians love their child - ren too. How

can I save my lit - tle boy from Op - pen - heim - er's dead - ly toy? There
is no his - tor - i - cal pre - ce - dent to put the words in the mouth of the pre - si - dent? There's

81

82

SEVEN DAYS

Words & Music by Sting

Sev - en days _____

will quick - ly go. _____ The

fact re - mains _____ I love her so. _____

Sev - en days, _____ so

Lyrics: It's a big e-nough um-brel - la, _____ but it's al-ways me __ that ends up get - ting wet, _____ yeah, yeah. ___

THIS COWBOY SONG

Words & Music by Sting

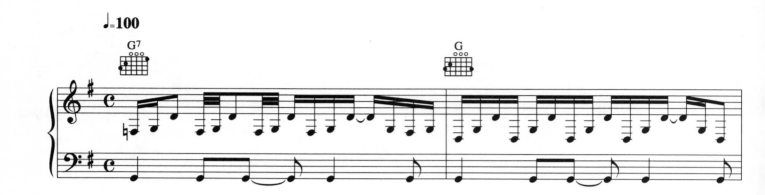

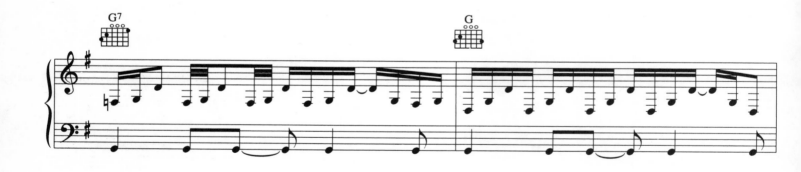

We rode all night a-cross an end - less de-sert,
(Verses 2, 3 & 4 see block lyric)

we had no moon to light our way. —

And though a mil - lion stars were slow - ly turn - ing,

1, 3.

we lacked the con - scien - ces to pray.

Coda

shin - ing   to - night.____   (ad lib.)

This cow - boy

song   is all I know   to bring me back   in - to   your arms,__

__ your dis - tant sun,   your shin - ing light,   you'll be my__

Verse 2:

Our horses running like a devil chase us
Their feet they hardly touch the ground
Yes I'm familiar with a grey wolf howling
But I'm certain I never heard that sound.

Verse 3:

I've been the lowest of the low on the planet
I've been a sinner all my days
When I was living with my hand on the trigger
I had no sense to change my ways.

Verse 4:

The preacher asked if I'd embrace the resurrection
To suck the poison from my life
Just like an existential cowboy villain
His words were balanced on my knife.

DEMOLITION MAN

Words & Music by Sting

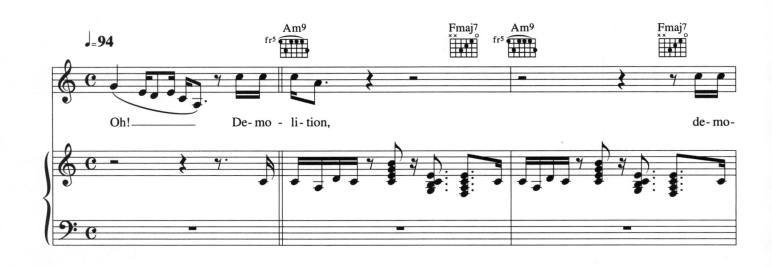

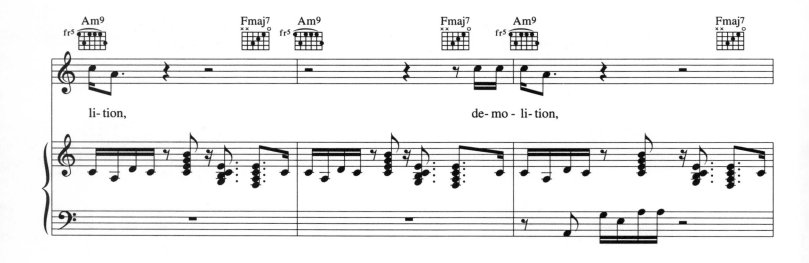

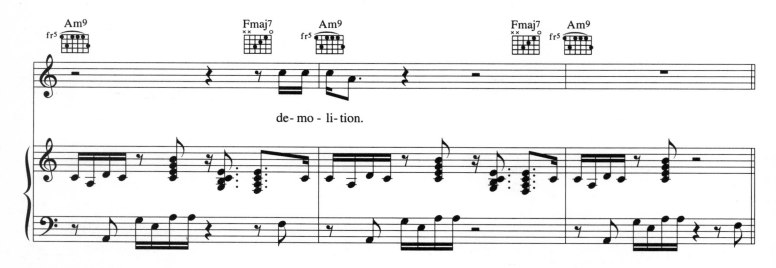

1. Tied to the tracks   and the train's fast com-ing,
(Verses 2 & 3 see block lyric)

strapped to the wing   with the en - gine run - ning.—

You say that this was-n't in your plan,—   don't mess a-round with the de-mo-li-tion man.

1.   **2.**

I'm a   walk-ing night-mare,   an ar-se-nal of doom, I

Verse 2:

Tied to a chair and the bomb is ticking

This situation is not of your picking

You say that this wasn't in your plan

Don't mess around with the demolition man.

Verse 3:

You come to me like a moth to the flame

It's love you need but I don't play that game

'Cause you could be my greatest fan

But I'm nobody's friend, I'm a demolition man.

11/95 (22861)